Snark! The Herald Angels Sing

Snark! The Herald Angels Sing

SARCASM, BITTERNESS, AND THE HOLIDAY SEASON

LAWRENCE DORFMAN

Skyhorse Publishing

Skyhorse Publishing books may be purchased in bulk at special discounts for sales promotion, corporate gifts, fund-raising, or educational purposes. Special editions can also be created to specifications. For details, contact the Special Sales Department, Skyhorse Publishing, 307 West 36th Street, 11th Floor, New York, NY 10018 or info@skyhorsepublishing.com.

Skyhorse® and Skyhorse Publishing® are registered trademarks of Skyhorse Publishing, Inc.®, a Delaware corporation.

www.skyhorsepublishing.com

10 9 8 7 6 5 4 3 2 1

Library of Congress Cataloging-in-Publication Data is available on file.
ISBN: 978-1-61608-422-6

Printed in China

This is a day of goodwill to all men, and the giving and receiving of presents which nobody particularly wants, a time for planned gaiety, determined sentiment and irrelevant expenses; a religious festival without religion; a commercialized orgy of love without a heart. Ah me! I fear I am becoming cynical, but how lovely would it be if it were an ordinary day when I could get on with my work and read and play.

—NOËL COWARD

CONTENTS

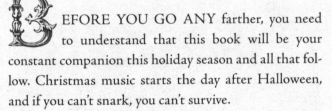**B**EFORE YOU GO ANY farther, you need to understand that this book will be your constant companion this holiday season and all that follow. Christmas music starts the day after Halloween, and if you can't snark, you can't survive.

I know. I've lumped together all the religions in this book. Not only that, but I'm including a smattering of Thanksgiving. One-stop shopping.

The title came to me in a dream.

Introduction

BAH! HUMBUG!

Has there ever been a time MORE suited to tapping into your inner snark?

No. Bar none, the number one, numero uno, absolute top spot for all things snark . . . belongs to the holidays.

Talk about your mixed emotions . . . the holidays—be they Christian, Jewish, African, or what have you—are truly the best and worst of times.[1]

This is a time of year when every single emotion you have in your body comes into play, when every last nerve is touched, fondled, and made to cry "Uncle." You will be stressed, stretched to the limit, distressed, disgusted, depressed, dejected, unhappy, unappreciated, and overwhelmed. There will be tears, sweat, and, occasionally, blood. It will be the constant juxtapositioning of

---

[1] Gonna be a lot of Dickens. Deal with it.

pleasure and pain. This had to be the Marquis de Sade's favorite time of the year.

Up until that moment when it all changes and you look around at your gathered loved ones, shout whatever sobriquet fits the occasion, hug and kiss each other, and smile profusely, all the while thinking to yourself, "Never again. I will not do this next year." But you will.

How to survive? Snark is the answer. Snark is the key. Snark is the way. In my other books, I told you, "Snark will set you free." Not so much here.

No, here, snark is a coping mechanism. A way to retain your sanity. A way to keep the wolves at bay (or at least out on the porch). A way to deal with relatives, shopping, rudeness, unleashed vitriolic bile that's been saved up for a year, wrapping, cooking, cleaning, decorating, shopping some more, writing out cards, making those myriad phone calls, sending out invitations, shopping yet again.

This is protection. This is a shield, like Superman's Fortress of Solitude. This is self-defense. This will stand up in court.

And while it is little consolation, you can take comfort in knowing that you're not alone. In one way or another, the entire world is going through the same thing.

Do you hear what I hear?

Merriment
(MARKETING)

IN WHICH THE AUTHOR INTRODUCES THE CRASS
COMMERCIALIZATION OF THE HOLIDAYS—SHOWS
THAT EVERY RELIGION EXPLOITS THEM IN A
DIFFERENT WAY—INTRODUCES SOME REDOUBTABLE
CHARACTERS WITH WHOM THE READER IS ALREADY
ACQUAINTED—AND DEMONSTRATES HOW SAID
RELIGIONS CAN LAY THEIR WORTHY HEADS TOGETHER

SO, WHAT'S IT ALL about, Alfie? Is it to celebrate THE birth? To bask in the miracle of a day's supply of oil that burned for eight? Is it to revel in the heritage of a continent, or start the year off with a clean slate?

Nah.

It's about sellin' stuff. It's about going so deep into debt so covertly you don't even know what you spent until tax time in April.

It's about MARKETING . . . and yes, I said it in all caps.

Food. Booze. More food. More booze. Toys. Clothes. Useless stuff. A little more useless stuff. A little MORE useless stuff. It's all about the "get."

"I don't know what to get for_____[fill in the blank]," which basically means, "What is he/she going to get me? How much do I have to spend back? What if they spent more? Will I feel bad? Hey, I deserve it. I was good this year."[2] Screw 'em. Last year I spent a lot, and all I got was an automated spaghetti twirler fork and a Scarface snow globe (which was actually a little cool, but all the snow had gone up Tony Montana's nose by the third shake, so . . .)

Anyway . . . shopping can be fun. In February. Wait until then.

In the meantime, it's here. Happy holidays. Noel. Peace on earth. Goodwill to whomever. Buckets of joy. Whatever.

All those presents, ingenious devices for taking money off you for things other people don't want in return for things you don't want yourself, in fact you often don't just not want them, you find them positively offensive. "So that's the kind of book/tie/bottle of booze/gadget they think I'd appreciate," you mutter aggrievedly.

—KINGSLEY AMIS

++

---

2   What's that even mean?

Christmas is the Disneyfication of Christianity.
—DON CUPITT

♦♦

Christmas is a race to see which gives out first—your
money or your feet.
—ANONYMOUS

♦♦♦

A Christmas shopper's complaint is
one of long-standing.
—JAY LENO

♦♦

For those of you out there who are thinking about
the Hanukkah-versus-Christmas thing, let me tell
you this: Quite honestly—and this comes from an
experiment with a two-and-a-half-year-old—Christmas
blows the doors off of Hanukkah.
—JON STEWART

♦♦♦

Hanukkah Books You'll Never See

➢ **The Schmuck Who Stole Hanukkah:** The story of a moron that tries to enter the village of Schvantzville to steal all the toys, but can't seem to pick the "big" night.

➢ **Good Night, Moon-orah:** A very *short* book, it follows a child on each night as she says good night to her presents. Chapter 1: "Good Night, Dreidel." End of chapter. Chapter 2: "Good Night, Chocolate Gelt in a Mesh Bag." End of chapter. And so on.

➢ **The Runaway Dreidel:** A dreidel wants to run away because everyone thinks he's just a cheap little top with writing on it.

➢ **The Giving Tree (But Just a Little):** A children's book that is instructional for parents, it tells the story of a little Jewish boy who befriends a tree and is institutionalized for it.

➢ **The Big Book of Mackabee Pop-ups:** Oy, too many swords. You'll put your eye out.

Oh look, yet another Christmas TV special! How
touching to have the meaning of Christmas brought
to us by cola, fast food, and beer . . . Who'd have
ever guessed that product consumption, popular
entertainment, and spirituality would
mix so harmoniously?
—BILL WATTERSON

✦✦✦

Anyone who believes that men are the equal of women
has never seen a man trying to wrap
a Christmas present.
—ANONYMOUS

✦✦

There is nothing sadder in this world than to wake
Christmas morning and not be a child.
—ERMA BOMBECK

✦✦✦

The three wise men sound very generous, but what
you've got to remember is that those gifts were joint
Christmas and birthday presents.
—JIMMY CARR

✦✦

Really Bad Holiday Ideas

1. Christmas ads with smoking Santas
2. Xmas cards with naked pics of you and family
3. Gifting a mausoleum for Christmas (just $10,000!)
4. Musical holly/wreaths/poinsettias
5. Mistletoe belt

I was so poor growing up if I hadn't been born a boy, I
would have had nothing to play with
on Christmas Day.
—RODNEY DANGERFIELD

♦♦

Nothing's as mean as giving a small child
something useful for Christmas.
—KIN HUBBARD

♦♦♦

Probably the worst thing about being Jewish during
Christmastime is shopping, because the lines are so
long. They should have a Jewish express line. "Look, I'm
a Jew. It's not a gift. It's just paper towels!"
—SUE KOLINSKY

••

The moment you stop believing in Santa Claus is the
moment you start getting clothes for Christmas.
—ANONYMOUS

•••

I'm giving everyone framed underwear for Christmas.
—ANDY WARHOL

••

Christmas: A day set apart and consecrated to gluttony,
drunkenness, maudlin sentiment, gift-taking, public
dullness and domestic behavior.
—AMBROSE BIERCE

•••

> **Tipping Notes**
>
> ➢ Thanks SO much for doing what you get paid for.
>
> ➢ Happy holidays. This is for another year of barely passable service.
>
> ➢ I appreciate the envelope with your name and address on it. Hard to reuse without a ton of Wite-Out, so here's a little somethin'...
>
> ➢ Happy Haveatcha and a merry guilt Trip.
>
> ➢ Here you are. Those ten hours of O. T. sure came in handy so I can do this for you.

There are a lot of things money can't buy. None of them are on my Christmas list.

—JOAN RIVERS

✦✦✦

One Christmas, things were so bad in our house that I asked Santa for a yo-yo and all I got was a piece of string. My father told me it was a yo.

—BRENDAN O'CARROLL

✦✦

Who says shopping early avoids the rush? I did mine a
full twelve months in advance, and the stores were just
as busy as ever.
—GAVIN MCKERNAN

✦✦✦

It makes one's mouth hurt to speak with
such forced merriment.
—DAVID SEDARIS

✦✦✦

My father gave me a bat for Christmas. The first time I
played with it, it flew away.
—RODNEY DANGERFIELD

✦✦✦

~✦~

*Phoebe: You know, Chandler, you being here is
the best gift I could ask for Christmas.
Chandler: Aw, thanks, Pheebs.
Phoebe: OK, now where's my real present?*
—FRIENDS

~✦~

12 Days of Gifts

1. Islamic Poker[3]
2. Fairly Serious Putty
3. The Lil' Electrical Outlet Licker
4. 5200 Card Pickup: a card game that keeps the kids busy all day
5. Ginsu Boomerang
6. The Pee-wee Herman Pull Toy
7. Nintendo 63 (This one was pretty easy to come by this holiday, for some reason.)
8. Hasbro's Lil' Barber
9. Tickle Me Carrot Top
10. Angry Birds-Baked-in-a-Pie
11. Doggie Dentist kit
12. The screenplay to the last *Star Trek* movie—"Live Long Then Expire"

---

[3]   Lose a hand? Lose a hand!

✦✦✦

Oh, joy . . . Christmas Eve. By this time
tomorrow, millions of people, knee-deep in
tinsel and wrapping paper, will utter those
heartfelt words, "Is this all I got?"
—*FRASIER*

✦✦

*For more than twenty-five years, Santa to the
Stars Brady White earned thousands of dollars
a night each December by playing Santa and
taking Christmas requests from the rich and
famous. White's most memorable moment?
Madonna sat on his lap one year and asked to
have her virginity back.*[4]

Christmas crept into Pine Cove like a creeping
Christmas thing: dragging garland, ribbon, and sleigh
bells, oozing eggnog, reeking of pine, and threatening
festive doom like a cold sore under the mistletoe.
—CHRISTOPHER MOORE

---

[4] Not even Santa can make that happen.

···

A lot of Americans got hi-definition televisions for Christmas, which means a lot more celebrities will be seeing their plastic surgeons this year.
—JOAN RIVERS

··

I bought my brother some gift-wrap for Christmas. I took it to the gift wrap department and told them to wrap it, but in a different print so he would know when to stop unwrapping.
—STEVEN WRIGHT

··

Santa asked the little girl what she wanted for Christmas.

"I want a Barbie and a G.I. Joe," said the girl.

"I thought Barbie comes with Ken?" asked Santa.

"No," she replied, "Barbie comes with G.I. Joe. She fakes it with Ken."

Christmas Facts

➤ A Christmas club, a savings account in which a person deposits a fixed amount of money regularly to be used at Christmas for shopping, came about around 1905. It is now a source of much amusement for bank employees when you get your bankbook and realize you could have made more interest with a lemonade stand.

➤ According to a 1995 survey, 7 out of 10 British dogs get Christmas gifts from their doting owners. That same survey revealed that only 5 of those 10 dogs actually return those gifts for something else.

➤ Although many believe the Friday after Thanksgiving is the busiest shopping day of the year, it is not. It is the fifth to tenth busiest day. It is, however, the day when the murder rate goes up significantly in almost 40 states.

Snarkin' the Holidays

➤ "Merry Christmas"—not "Happy Holidays" or "Season's Greetings"—is once again OK to use.

➤ "Family trees"? Or worse, "holiday trees"? Not on my watch.

➤ What about Christmas songs? "Have Yourself a Merry Little Day of Winter"? "Frosty the Snowperson"? Or "Deck the Halls with Boughs of Unendangered Foliage"?

➤ You couldn't give a "bum" a handout for "the holidays" anymore . . . no, no, he's a *displaced person.*

➤ "Gee, Daddy, Santa Claus is really fat!" . . . "No, sweetie, he's got an *enlarged physical condition caused by a completely natural genetically induced hormonal imbalance.*"

➤ "Look, Mom, an elf!" . . . "Now, now, that man is just *Vertically Challenged.*"

> Tip the janitor? No, no, no . . . he's a *custodial artist*. Double whatever you were gonna give him.

Go ahead, say what you want, because it's beginning to feel a lot like that short period of time in December.

—THE AUTHOR

~•~

Stan: Yeah, and you know, I think I learned something today. It doesn't matter if you're Christian or Jewish or atheist or Hindu. Christmas, still, is about one very important thing—
Cartman: Yeah, ham.
Stan: Christmas is about something much more important.
Kyle: What?
Stan: Presents.
Kyle: Hey man, if you're Jewish, you get presents for eight days!
Stan: Wow, really? Count me in!
Cartman: Yeah, I'll be a Jew too!

—SOUTH PARK

~•~

Traditions
(SPIRIT)

IN WHICH THE AUTHOR TRIES TO FIND THE TRUE
MEANING OF THE HOLIDAYS AND FAILS MISERABLY—
LOOKS TO THE AGES FOR GUIDANCE AND FINDS NO ONE
AT HOME—EXPLORES THE SURROUNDING HOLIDAYS
FOR SUSTENANCE AND LEAVES THE TABLE HUNGRY—
AND ULTIMATELY CONCLUDES THAT THE WAY OF THE
SNARK IS THE ONLY RIGHTEOUS ONE

EVEN IF YOU DON'T spend a single minute entertaining people in your home, you're still going to find yourself putting up decorations, cleaning the house, readying it for the holidays . . . and if there's an obsessive/compulsive in your life, you might as well just call it a day now.

We all know the type. Those extremely annoying people who just "absolutely, positively ADORE the holidays!" . . . who spend thousands of dollars on lights and decorations that you can see from the space shuttle, who have their shopping and cooking done by the first week of October ("I'm completely done, so I can just enjoy every moment of time this year!") . . . and have a three-month supply of obnoxious snowman or Christmas tree or reindeer sweaters so they can wear one every day. You know, those morons who feel the spirit

SO intensely they have to have Santa legs sticking out from the trunk of their car, or a wreath in every window, or put antlers on the hood or, even worse, on their head right after Thanksgiving and don't take them off until New Year's Day. Remember, it's still deer season, so if I see antlers, I may shoot to kill.

There should be a place for those people—a big warehouse club–like structure where they can go and frenzy themselves into a holiday stupor—but alas, there is none, so load up on these snarks and have at it. They'll thank you in the end. Or, at least, everyone else will.

I have long thought it a pity that Scrooge, like so many people in Dickens, spoilt his case by overstatement. To dismiss the Christmas spirit as humbug will not quite do as it stands, but it gets close.
—KINGSLEY AMIS

✦✦✦

Mail your packages early so the post office can lose them in time for Christmas.
—JOHNNY CARSON

✦✦

~•~

Frasier: Dad, what are you doing with that wreath?
Martin: I'm gonna hang it on the door like I always do.
Frasier: But it's plastic!
Martin: Of course it's plastic! Do you think a real one would have lasted since 1967?
—FRASIER

~•~

Last Christmas, I put up stockings.
All I got were Odor Eaters.
—RODNEY DANGERFIELD

•••

In the immortal words of Tiny Tim,
"God help us everyone!"
—GROUCHO MARX

••

Most Texans think Hanukkah is some
sort of duck call.
—RICHARD LEWIS

•••

I got a sweater for Christmas . . . I wanted a screamer
or a moaner.

++

Kiss her under the mistletoe? I wouldn't
kiss her under anesthetic.

+++

I've learned that you can tell a lot about a person by the
way (s)he handles these three things: a rainy day, lost
luggage, and tangled Christmas tree lights.
—MAYA ANGELOU

++

If "ifs" and "buts" were candy and nuts, wouldn't it be a
merry Christmas?
—DON MEREDITH

+++

Well, what shall we hang, the holly
or each other?
—HENRY II, *THE LION IN WINTER*

++

Brain Scan: Inside the Head of a Snowman

> I'm dreaming of a white Christmas . . .
> I'm dreaming of a white Christmas . . .
> I'm dreaming of a white Christmas . . .

> I'm dreaming of a white Christmas . . .
> I'm dreaming of a white Christmas . . .
> I'm dreaming of a white Christmas . . .

> I'm dreaming of a white Christmas . . .
> I'm dreaming of a white Christmas . . .
> I'm dreaming of a white Christmas . . .

Christmas Is . . .

A time for saying that Christmas is a time for doing things that one should, frankly, be doing anyway. "Christmas is a time for considering people less fortunate than ourselves." Oh, July and August aren't, is that it?
—STEPHEN FRY

••

A time when people of all religions come together to worship Jesus Christ.
—BART SIMPSON, *THE SIMPSONS*

•••

Hell in a stupid sweater.
—CARINA CHOCANO

••

Santa Claus and elves and stockings hung by the fireplace and good cheer and a big dinner and sugar cookies and gifts, gifts and more gifts.
—BINNIE KIRSHENBAUM

•••

The collectivization of gaiety and the compulsory infliction of joy.
—CHRISTOPHER HITCHENS

••

The magical time of year when
all your money disappears.
—HAL ROACH

✦✦✦

Awesome. First of all, you get to spend time with the
ones you love. Secondly, you can get drunk and no one
can say anything. Third, you give presents. What's
better than giving presents? And fourth, getting
presents. So four things. Not bad for one day. It's really
the greatest day of all.
—MICHAEL SCOTT, *THE OFFICE*

✦✦

People being helped by people other than me.
—JERRY SEINFELD

✦✦✦

Tradition. That's what you associate with Christmas:
tradition. And drunk driving. And despair and
lonliness. But mainly tradition.
—CHARLIE BROOKER

✦✦

George Bernard Shaw

↔ I am sorry to have to introduce the subject of Christmas. It's an indecent subject; a cruel, gluttonous subject; a drunken, disorderly subject; a wasteful, disastrous subject; a wicked, cadging, lying, filthy, blasphemous and demoralizing subject. Christmas is forced on a reluctant and disgusted nation by the shopkeepers and the press: on its own merits it would wither and shrivel in the fiery breath of universal hatred; and anyone who looked back to it would be turned into a pillar of greasy sausages.

↔ It is really an atrocious institution. We must be gluttonous because it is Christmas. We must be drunken because it is Christmas. . . . We must buy things that nobody wants and give them to people we don't like; because the mass of the population, including the all-powerful middle-class tradesman, depends on a week of license and brigandage, waste and intemperance, to clear off its outstanding liabilities at the end of the year. . . . As for me, I shall fly from it all tomorrow.

↔ Like all intelligent people, I greatly dislike Christmas. It revolts me to see a whole nation refrain from music for weeks together in order that every man may rifle his neighbor's pockets under cover of a ghastly pretense of festivity.

↔ A perpetual holiday is a good working definition of hell.

"The Little Drummer Boy" was playing in the background for what seemed like the third time in a row. I fought off an urge to beat that Little Drummer Boy senseless with his own drumsticks.
—DANA REINHARDT

++

A Northern man was traveling through a small southern town when he found a "Nativity scene" that was created with great skill and talent. The only strange thing was that the three wise men were wearing firemen's helmets.

Totally unable to come up with a reason or explanation, he stopped at a 7-Eleven at the edge of town and asked the lady behind the counter about the helmets.

She exploded into a rage, yelling, "You darn Yankees never read your bibles!"

The man said he had read the Bible many times, but couldn't recall any mention of firemen.

She jerked her Bible from behind the counter and riffled through some pages, and finally jabbed her finger at a passage. "See, it says right here, 'The three wise man came from afar.'"

The Italian version? One Mary, one
Jesus, 33 wise guys.
—ANONYMOUS

❖❖

Jeez, why are we talking about God and religion? It's
Christmas!
—JACKIE, *ROSEANNE*

❖❖❖

*A woman goes to the post office to buy stamps
for her Hanukkah cards. She says to the clerk,
"May I have 50 Hanukkah stamps?" The clerk
says, "What denomination?" The woman says,
"Oh my god. Has it come to this? Give me 6
Orthodox, 12 Conservative, and 32 Reform."*

Being prepared is the secret of a harmonious
Christmas. If Joseph had booked ahead, Jesus would
not have been born in a stable.
—JILLY COOPER

❖❖

~•~

Lucy: Merry Christmas, Charlie Brown. At this time of the year, I think we should put aside our differences and try to be kind.

Charlie Brown: Why does it have to be just this time of year? Can't it be all year round?

Lucy: What are you? Some kind of fanatic or something?

—PEANUTS

~•~

It is my heart-warmed and world-embracing Christmas hope and aspiration that all of us, the high, the low, the rich, the poor, the admired, the despised, the loved, the hated, the civilized, the savage, may eventually be gathered together in a heaven of everlasting rest and peace and bliss, except the inventor of the telephone.

—MARK TWAIN

•••

During the first day of Hanukkah, two elderly Jewish men were sitting in a wonderful deli frequented almost exclusively by Jews in New York City. They were talking among themselves in Yiddish—the colorful language of Jews who came over from Eastern Europe.

A Chinese waiter, in New York for only a year, came up and in fluent, impeccable Yiddish asked them if everything was OK and if they were enjoying the holiday.

The Jewish men were dumbfounded. "Where did he ever learn such perfect Yiddish?" they both thought. After they paid the bill, they asked the restaurant manager, an old friend of theirs, "Where did our waiter learn such fabulous Yiddish?"

The manager looked around and leaned in so no one else would hear and said, "Shhhh. He thinks we're teaching him English."

Three men die in a car accident Christmas Eve. They all find themselves at the pearly gates waiting to enter heaven. On entering they must present something "Christmassy."

The first man searches his pocket and finds some mistletoe, so he is allowed in.

The second man presents some holly, so he is also allowed in.

The third man pulls out a pair of panties.

Confused at this last gesture, St. Peter asks, "How do these represent Christmas?"

The third man answers "They're Carol's."

Roses are reddish / Violets are bluish / If it weren't for Christmas / We'd all be Jewish.
—BENNY HILL

••

December 25 is National Jews Go to the Movies Day.
—JON STEWART

•••

Snarkin' the Holidays

Finally, out of the mall. Takes an hour, but it's good to be out and on the highway—which, frankly, isn't a whole lot better than the parking lot, but I see freedom. My heart rate slows, and my breathing becomes more regular. We've made it. We're free. That's when I hear those dreaded words: "Remember, the Yablonskis asked us to stop by for a drink."

I want to stop by and have a drink with *them* like I want to cough up a lung.

The after-shopping-just-drop-by drink is like dancing in a body cast. I mean, it's dancing. It should be fun, but it just doesn't quite make it. And the Yablonskis and their ilk are people who usually brag about having all their shopping finished. Their house is decorated with thousands of stuffed rats in Christmas garb. (What the hell is that about?) Their tree is perfect. They have a perfect roaring fire and warm brandy liquor laced with . . . I don't know, honey or lemon. (Because you can't find a better way to screw up liquor?)

I hate this. I am in hell.

—THE AUTHOR

Christmas Facts

➢ "Hot cockles" was a popular game at Christmas in medieval times. It was a game in which the other players took turns striking the blindfolded player, who had to guess the name of the person delivering each blow. Hot cockles was still a Christmas pastime until the Victorian era and has only recently been reintroduced as a method of preparation for holiday shopping.

➢ According to the National Christmas Tree Association, Americans buy 37.1 million real Christmas trees each year. On January 2, the National Waste Management Association claims it picks up almost 36.9 million of said trees.

> After *A Christmas Carol*, Charles Dickens wrote several other Christmas stories, one each year, but none were as successful as the original. Among the least successful were *A Christmas Mildred*, *A Christmas Agnes*, and *A Christmas Bob*. Additionally, before settling on the name Tiny Tim, Dickens considered three other alliterative names: Little Larry, Puny Pete, Small Sam, Miniscule Marty, Wee Willie, and Malnourished Mark. Never had a chance.

> An average household in America will mail out 28 Christmas cards each year and see 28 eight cards return in their place. Because if you get 27 back this year, you're mailing out 27 cards next year.

President Obama held a ceremony at the White House to celebrate the first night of Hanukkah. In response, Republicans said, "It's even worse than we thought. He's a Jewish Muslim."
—CONAN O'BRIEN

✦✦✦

Did you ever notice that life seems to follow certain patterns? Like I noticed that every year around this time, I hear Christmas music.
—TOM SIMS

✦✦

Let's Go A-Caroling

➢ ALL I WANT FOR CHRISTMAS IS MY TWO FRONT TEETH. (On Amy Winehouse's Christmas list)

➢ ANGELS WE HAVE HEARD ON HIGH. (High on what? Angel dust? Nyuk, nyuk.)

➢ CHESTNUTS ROASTING ON AN OPEN FIRE. (Don't sit so close to the fire, you moron.)

➤ DO YOU HEAR WHAT I HEAR? (Really? I mean, really? You'd think you'd know better. Tell the world, go ahead. Damn gossip.)

➤ FROSTY THE SNOWMAN (Drug dealer)

➤ GOD REST YE MERRY, GENTLEMEN (Party 'til you die.)

➤ HAVE YOURSELF A MERRY LITTLE CHRISTMAS (I'm tapped out.)

➤ HERE WE COME A-WASSAILING (You ever see a body trampled by a herd of wassails? Not pretty.)

➤ LET IT SNOW! LET IT SNOW! LET IT SNOW! (Followed by the lesser-known LET ME SHOVEL! LET ME SHOVEL! LET ME DIE OF A HEART ATTACK!

➤ ROCKIN' AROUND THE CHRISTMAS-TREE (Don't come a-knockin' if the Christmas tree is rockin'!)

➤ RUDOLPH THE RED-NOSED REIN-DEER (Nothing worse than a boozing reindeer. They miss the roof, leave cookie crumbs, and crap where they want to.)

- ➤ SANTA BABY (Guess he went down more than the chimney.)

- ➤ SANTA CLAUS IS COMING TO TOWN & HERE COMES SANTA CLAUS (Santa got Viagra for Christmas, didn't he?)

- ➤ SILENT NIGHT (Yeah, like you can keep your mouth shut.)

- ➤ TWELVE DAYS OF CHRISTMAS (Cost me over a hundred grand to make this happen last year. Never again. The Leaping Lords stayed until mid-February.)

- ➤ WE THREE KINGS (Larry, Don, and Nosmo)

- ➤ WHAT CHILD IS THIS? (He doesn't look like me. I want a paternity test . . . now!)

- ➤ WHITE CHRISTMAS (Peruvian flake. Merry Christmas, yo.)

I'm so riddled with the holiday spirit that the mere
mention of stocking filler sexually arouses me.
—JOHN WATERS

◆◆◆

Celebrities love the season of goodwill to all men. No
need to put up Christmas lights—they just crank up
the power on the electric fence until it's white hot.
—DAVID LETTERMAN

◆◆

On the first night of Hanukkah, Jewish parents do
something that can only be described as sadistic when
they hand their child a top. A top. To play with. They
call this top a dreidel. I know a fuckin' top when I
see one. You can call it the king's nuts, I don't give a
shit. Call it whatever you like, it's a top. A top is not
something you play with. A top is not a toy. A toy
is something you participate with. It'd be like the
equivalent of if you had a young girl and she wanted a
Barbie and you handed her a stick and said
give it a name.
—LEWIS BLACK

◆◆◆

Snarkin' the Holidays

Christmas movies have pretty much always sucked. Completely filled with schmaltz and saccharin, and usually diabetic coma worthy, they also are clearly an exploitative moment when the filmmakers decided, "The hell with story, the hell with plot, I'm gettin' paid!" and make movies that are bland or boring or just plain bad.

"But Snark . . . I love [fill in the blank]!"

Yes, I know, there ARE a handful out there that never fail to tug at your heartstrings and that signal a beginning to the season . . . a season that really NEEDS something to jump-start the mood. *It's a Wonderful Life*, the original *Miracle on 34th Street*, *A Charlie Brown Christmas*, the cartoon version of *How the Grinch Stole Christmas*—these are all terrific flicks. They can change your mood in an instant, even if you've seen them a hundred times.

But because they've hit a note in our collective psyche, every studio in Hollywood has tried to find a new replacement for these movies and 99 percent of the dreck that's resulted has failed miserably.

Here's a smattering of the Worst of the Worst:

➢ *Ernest Saves Christmas* – A yokel Christmas, based on a character that should have had the shelf life of a bunch of bananas. Santa's chauffeur? Really? This crapfest took about three minutes to conceptualize and slightly less to write.

➢ *Jack Frost* – Dead parent reincarnated as a live snowman. Yep. Could happen. Just no bonding nights around the fireplace, right? Oh wait, what's that you say? A Christmas miracle? Right. The only miracle here is that the filmmakers ever worked again.

➢ *Jingle All the Way* – The movie that comes closest to capturing the "real" spirit of Christmas: Get what you need at all costs. Fatherly love as shown through the procurement of an impossible-to-get action figure. Pit the dad against a stressed-out postal worker for the last one anywhere and watch the hilarity ensue. Starring Ahhnold, so you may need to use the subtitles.

➢ *All I Want for Christmas* – Starring Leslie Neilsen of *Naked Gun* fame, this one wanted to be the *Home Alone* of holiday movies, and failed miserably. (Some might put *Home Alone* on the list as a holiday movie . . . nope. While successful, the original and it's sequels never quite accomplished mood changer status.) There is a good lesson to be learned, however: Kidnapping Santa is never a good way to bring your divorced parents back together.

➢ *Santa Claus Conquers the Martians* – Made in 1964, this movie tried to capitalize on the fear of alien life and extraterrestrials that had begun to build in the public. And if you're drunk enough or high enough, this movie can also be quite funny. It also begs audience participation, like the *The Rocky Horror Picture Show* . . . but I'm a little afraid of what you might want to throw instead of rice.

➢ *Eight Crazy Nights* – Adam Sandler's homage to Hanukkah. Even at a scant seventy-one minutes, this one is seventy-one minutes too long. There's enough scatalogical references and sophomoric humor to make it feel like it takes eight hours to watch.

> ➤ **Fred Claus** – Santa's dumber yet craftier older brother. When he gets in trouble, Nick bails him out. But he has to promise servitude at the North Pole . . . yikes. Where's Dr. Phil when you need him?

The last movie above actually leads into a subcategory group. It stars Vince Vaughn, who seems to have latched on to the whole holiday-means-box-office premise. So when you're on Netflix or at the video store, looking for that one movie that will help you find the spirit and the mood, here's another rule of thumb for your viewing protection:

No Vince Vaughn movies . . . no Ben Affleck movies . . . no Tim Allen movies . . . and beware Jim Carrey.

All have done multiple Christmas flicks and all are bad.

So rent the good ones again, make yourself a cup of nog and some popcorn, snuggle in, and watch for that moment when Clarence gets his wings or when Natalie gets her dream house . . . and be thankful you didn't opt for *The Santa Clause . . . part 3*, no less—now THAT'S a Christmas miracle.

Don't even get me started on television . . .

—THE AUTHOR

Christmas cards are just junk mail from people
you know.
—PATRICIA MARX

··

If you don't know about Hanukkah, I'll give you a brief
little history. Hanukkah was conceived in 1957 by an
optometrist in Nova Scotia, Dr. Maurice Tarnouer.
And a lot of people think it's some sort of answer to
Christmas to appease children who see their more
powerful, affluent Christian friends able to celebrate
this day. And they think it was somehow invented to
appease those kids and say, "Well, you know, us Jews
have our own thing. Here's eight days, so fuck you—
how 'bout that?" And people who believe that
are correct.
—DAVID CROSS

···

Roses are things which Christmas is not a bed of.
—OGDEN NASH

··

When decorating the tree, always use strings of cheap
lights manufactured in Third World nations that only
recently found out about electricity and have no words
in their language for "fire code."
—DAVE BARRY

••

Christmas: Holiday in which the past or the future are
not of as much interest as the present.

•••

Christmas is a holiday that persecutes the lonely, the
frayed, and the rejected.
—JIMMY CANNON

••

When you compare Christmas to Hannukkah,
Christmas is great. Hannukkah sucks! First night you
get socks. Second night, an eraser, a notebook. It's a
Back-to-School holiday!
—LEWIS BLACK

•••

Four Reasons Hanukkah Sucks

1. **No good cards:** Rows and rows of Christmas cards and only one row of Hanukkah cards. Yeah, like you've got a hundred different people you want to send Hanukkah cards to . . . well, you'd better get them out in time because, after all, there only are EIGHT DAYS ON WHICH THEY CAN BE DELIVERED. The best Hanukkah card ever? "It's not your fault that Hanukkah sucks." End of story.

2. **The name:** Too many ways to spell and pronounce the name of the holiday. Yeah, I know. It's hard to say. Sounds funny too. Like you've got something stuck in your throat. And oy, boychick, is it hard to spell. Gee, is it *Hanukah* or *Chanuka* or *Chanukah* or *Chanukkah* or *Channukah* or *Hanukah* or *Hannukah* or *Hanukkah* or *Hanuka* or *Hanukka* or *Hanaka* or *Haneka* or *Hanika* or *Khanukkah* . . . Please kill me now?

3. **Bad gifts:** Small. Large. Two medium. Small again. Large. Nothing. Small. Large(ish). Let's face it, Jewish parents don't really have much imagination. Not their fault. They've been struggling forever in

the shadow of the Big One. For years. Their parents had the same problem. It's up to you to stop the madness.

4. **The music:** I once heard a story that Irving Berlin hated "White Christmas." Whattya wanna bet that that rumor got started by somebody who was pissed off that the only music associated with this holiday are a lame Adam Sandler ditty that's just dumb . . . and the dreidel song.

Family
(HELL)

**IN WHICH THE AUTHOR ALIENATES EVERYONE WHO
SHARES HIS BLOOD LINE—DEALS WITH MYRIAD
PERSONAL QUESTIONS ABOUT MARRIAGE, LOVE LIFE,
SEXUAL ORIENTATION—CONJURES UP EVERY SLIGHT,
MEAN WORD, OR PECCADILLO THAT'S BEEN HIDDEN
AWAY ALL YEAR—ALL IN THE NAME OF CHRISTMAS
SPIRIT, LOVE, AND BONDING**

WHEN YOU GO HOME, you're going to have to see people you'd just as soon avoid. For many people, that's pretty much your entire extended family.

Everybody has an uncle, aunty, brother, or cousin who doesn't know his/her limits . . . or that wine and vodka and painkillers are a bad combination . . . who then puts his/her arms around you, sits you down on the couch, and talks incoherently to you for hours, all the while blowing that heady combo of alcohol breath (mixed with onion dip) into your face. You can't get away fast enough.

You feel guilty. You're definitely not happy to see them and couldn't be less interested in what they have to say, but they are family.[5] You can't even muster a fake

---

5   Keep reminding yourself. Over and over.

smile and start to amuse yourself by muttering asides that would make Andrew Dice Clay blush. Ah . . . there's the snark. Is it working?

If you want to restore your faith in humanity, think about Christmas. If you want to destroy it again, think about Christmas shopping. But the gifts aren't the important thing about the holidays. The important thing is having your family around resenting you.
—RENO GOODALE

··

My mom wanted to know why I never get home for the holidays. I said, "Because I can't get Delta to wait in the yard while I run in."
—MARGARET SMITH

···

I believed in Christmas until I was eight years old. I had saved up some money and was going to buy my mother a clothes boiler. I kept the money hidden in a brown crock in the coal bin. My father found it and stole the money. Ever since then I have remembered nobody on Christmas, and I want nobody to remember me.
—W. C. FIELDS

A little boy wrote to Santa Claus "Please send me a sister."

Santa Claus wrote him back, "OK, send me your mother."

I once bought my kids a set of batteries for Christmas with a note on it saying, toys not included.
—BERNARD MANNING

A menopausal mother and an electric carving knife? Not a good combination.
—JENNY ÉCLAIR

For the holidays, I bought my mother a self-complaining oven.
—RICHARD LEWIS

◆◆

I hate Christmas. . . . I am an atheist—thank God . . . the hypocrisy of it all, it is a shopkeeper's delight. I see women who are panicked by the kids spending money they can't afford on crap that will only be thrown away. The murder rate goes up at Christmas. Most families hate each other and can't wait to say piss off.
—WARREN MITCHELL

◆◆◆

No self-respecting mother would run out of intimidations on the eve of a major holiday.
—ERMA BOMBECK

◆◆

Everyone thinks I'm Jewish. I'm not. Last year I got a call: "Happy Hanukkah." I said, "Ma, I'm not Jewish."
—JOY BEHAR

◆◆◆

A Bubbie was giving directions to her grown grandson who was coming to visit for Hanukkah with his wife.

"You come to the front door of the apartment complex. You'll see a big panel at the door. With your elbow push button 14T. I will buzz you in."

"OK, got it."

"No, there's more. When you come inside, the elevator is on the right. Get in and with your elbow hit 14. When you get out, I am on the left. With your elbow, hit my doorbell."

"Grandma, that sounds easy," replied the grandson, "but why am I hitting all these buttons with my elbow?"

To which she answered, "What, you're coming empty-handed?"

6 Festive Ways to Drive Your Family Crazy

> ➢ Go to the mall with your mom and sit on Santa's lap. Refuse to get off.
> ➢ Claim you were a Christmas tree in your former life. When your dad tries to bring one into the room, scream bloody murder and thrash on the floor.
> ➢ Hang a stocking with your sister's name on it and fill it with coal. When she asks, say, "You've been very naughty this year."
> ➢ Build a snowman with your brother and place a hat on its head. If it doesn't come to life, start crying, "It didn't work!"
> ➢ Stand in front of the mirror reciting "How the Grinch Stole Christmas" over and over in your underwear.
> ➢ Wake up the house every morning by singing, "He sees you when you're sleeping . . ."

This, after all, was the month in which families began tightening and closing and sealing; from Thanksgiving to the New Year, everybody's world contracted, day by day, into the microcosmic single festive household, each with its own rituals and obsessions, rules and dreams. You didn't feel you could call people. They didn't feel they could phone you. How does one cry for help from these seasonal prisons?

—ZADIE SMITH

••

Marry an orphan: You'll never have to spend boring holidays with the in-laws (at most, an occasional visit to the cemetery).

—GEORGE CARLIN

•••

When I was little, my grandfather gave me a box of broken glass for Christmas. He gave my brother a box of Bandaids and said, "You two share."

—STEVEN WRIGHT

••

My parents, my whole life, combined my birthday with
Christmas, and you know how frustrating that is for a
child—especially as I was born in July.
—RITA RUDNER

✦✦✦

My husband is so cheap. On Christmas Eve he fires one
shot and tells the kids Santa committed suicide.
—PHYLLIS DILLER

✦✦

Christmas always sucked when I was a kid because
I believed in Santa Claus. Unfortunately, so did my
parents. So I never got anything.
—CHARLIE VIRACOLA

✦✦✦

The worst part of Christmas is dinner with the family,
when you realize how truly mutated and crippled is the
gene stock from which you sprang.
—BYRON ROGERS

✦✦

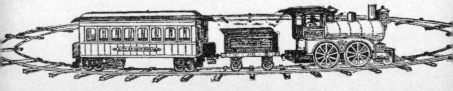

We're having the same old thing for Christmas dinner
this year . . . relatives.
—MARK TWAIN

++

Last Christmas, I gave my kid a BB gun. He gave me a
sweatshirt with a bull's-eye on the back.
—RODNEY DANGERFIELD

+++

I'm still keeping my New Year's resolutions. I only
make one because it's the only one easy to keep; I
resolve to spend less time with my family.
—MARIA MENOZZI

++

Thanksgiving. It's like we didn't even try to come up
with a tradition. The tradition is, we overeat. "Hey,
how about at Thanksgiving we just eat a lot?" "But
we do that every day!" "Oh. What if we eat a lot with
people that annoy the hell out of us?"
—JIM GAFFIGAN

+++

A man in Phoenix calls his son in New York the day before Hanukkah and says, "I hate to ruin your day, but I have to tell you that your mother and I are divorcing. Forty-five years of misery is enough."

"Pop, what are you talking about?" the son screams.

"We can't stand the sight of each other any longer," the father says. "We're sick of each other, and I'm sick of talking about this, so you call your sister in Chicago and tell her."

Frantic, the son calls his sister, who explodes on the phone. "Like heck they're getting divorced," she shouts. "I'll take care of this." She calls Phoenix immediately and screams at her father, "You are NOT getting divorced. Don't do a single thing until I get there. I'm calling New York, and we'll both be there tomorrow. Until then, don't do a thing, DO YOU HEAR ME?"

The old man hangs up his phone and turns to his wife. "OK," he says, "they're coming for Hanukkah and paying their own way."

My family wasn't very religious. On Hanukkah, they had a menorah on a dimmer.
—RICHARD LEWIS

◆◆◆

The one thing women don't want to find in their stockings on Christmas morning is their husband.
—JOAN RIVERS

◆◆

Christmas, it seems to me, is a necessary festival; we require a season when we can regret all the flaws in our human relationships: It is the feast of failure, sad but consoling.
—GRAHAM GREENE

◆◆◆

Christmas is a time when you get homestick—even when you're home.
—CAROL NELSON

◆◆

I looked in my mom's closet and saw what I was getting for Christmas . . . an UltraVibe Pleasure 2000.
—ERIC CARTMAN, *SOUTH PARK*

◆◆◆

10 of the Worst Gifts for Kids

1. Lottery scratch-offs
2. Knitted sweater and socks set (that are connected to each other)
3. French fry-o-lator
4. An assortment of maps
5. Membership in a food co-op
6. 10-count of dental floss from Costco
7. A fur (fake, of course) toilet seat cover
8. An address book, already filled in
9. Jane Fonda workout tapes
10. A Chia-Rat

It is customarily said that Christmas is done "for the kids." Considering how awful Christmas is and how little our society likes children, this must be true.
—P. J. O'ROURKE

++

Santa Claus has the right idea. Visit people once a year.
—VICTOR BORGE

+++

The one thing I remember about Christmas was that
my father used to take me out in a boat about ten miles
offshore on Christmas Day, and I used to have to swim
back. Extraordinary. It was a ritual. Mind you, that
wasn't the hard part. The difficult bit was getting out
of the sack.
—JOHN CLEESE

✦✦

The thought of Christmas overwhelms him. He no
longer looks forward to the holiday; he wants only to be
on the other side of the season. His impatience makes
him feel that he is incontrovertibly, finally, an adult.
—JHUMPA LAHIRI

✦✦✦

Thanksgiving is an emotional time. People travel
thousands of miles to be with the people they see only
once a year. And then discover that once a year is way
too often.
—JOHNNY CARSON

✦✦

The Office
(WORK)

IN WHICH THE AUTHOR EXPLORES THE PITFALLS
OF FORCED INTIMACY, CONFINED JOCULARITY, AND
REQUIRED BROTHERHOOD—SHOWS THE ERROR IN
THE WAY OF OVERINDULGENCE—AND WARNS OF A
HEINOUS DANGER THAT LIES BEHIND EVERY FILE
CABINET

"**D**ID I REALLY SAY that? Did I really DO that?"

Man, those sentences carry with them the weight of the world and all the remorse, fear, and embarrassment that can be mustered by someone who has absolutely no idea what happened. . . .

And the catalyst for all this angst? The Office Party.

Yes, it's that time of year again when reason and logic lock themselves away in that file cabinet with the drawer that sticks . . . when decorum and common sense head to Jamaica for the holidays . . . when your real self leaves your body and is replaced by a demon that can't drink enough, party hard enough, or say enough stupid things to last an entire career—a demon that is The Exorcist, Damian, and Freddy Kruger rolled into one, and that wipes out everything great you've done in the year before it.

Here's the thing (and write this down and refer to it—before you go to the party and at every bathroom break): No matter how cool you think you are, the Office Party is NOT the place you're going to prove it to everybody. Especially after a half dozen drinks.

You must be careful. There are pitfalls, traps, and danger around every corner. You may do or say something that you will never live down—something so heinous that it may get you put on probation, warned, or even fired . . . and could follow you and haunt you throughout the rest of your career.

But y'all have fun now, hear?

Christmas begins about the first of December with an office party and ends when you finally realize what you spent, around April fifteenth of the next year.
—P. J. O'ROURKE

++

Christmas is a time when everybody wants his past forgotten and his present remembered. What I don't like about office Christmas parties is looking for a job the next day.
—PHYLLIS DILLER

+++

Well, he keeps telling me he wants "skinny jeans"
so . . . Cheese of the Month Club.
—LIZ LEMON, ABOUT PETE'S SECRET SANTA GIFT,
30 ROCK

••

8 Christmas Things Not to Say to Your Boss

1. Did you get anything under the tree?
2. I think your balls are hanging too low.
3. Check out Rudolph's honker!
4. Santa's sack is really bulging.
5. Lift up the skirt so I can get to the bottom.
6. I love licking the end till it's really sharp and pointy.
7. From here, you can't tell if they're real or artificial.
8. To get it to stand up straight, try propping it against
    the wall.

~•~

*Jane Hathaway: If you would only display a
little generosity: a Christmas bonus, a few gifts!
Milburn Drysdale: I refuse to commercialize
Christmas just to kowtow to my pampered
employees.*

—*THE BEVERLY HILLBILLIES*

~•~

At an Office Party, Remember . . .

➢ You are not a stripper.

➢ You are not the "life of the party."

➢ You are not James Bond.

➢ You are not the world's greatest lover.

➢ The boss's wife is not hot for you.

➢ Suggesting a threesome is not a good idea.

➢ It is not cool to drink out of your shoe.

➢ Photocopying your buttocks, drilling a hole in the wall to the ladies' room, and shoving crudites into the mail slots will never be funny.

➢ Peeing on a computer is a FEDERAL offense.

➢ Fashionably late is just late.

➢ Your snowman sweater is just dumb, not ironic.

➢ Ditto for your reindeer antler headband.

➢ Ranting about "The True Meaning of Christmas" could[6] get you beaten up in the parking lot.

---

[6] (and should)

At the Christmas office party, you're supposed to sit naked on the copier machine, not the shredder.
—DAVID LETTERMAN

••

Yikes. You moon one person at an office party and suddenly you're not "professional" anymore?
—ANONYMOUS

•••

There's always some amount of gradual, slow burning destruction over the course of partying.
—GAVIN DEGRAW

••

Partying is such sweet sorrow.
—ROBERT BYRNE

•••

Q: Why is Christmas just like a day at the office?
A: You do all the work, and the fat guy with the suit gets all the credit.

What NOT to Say at Office Xmas Parties

- Man, your wife is smokin' hot—bet you get a ton of UPS deliveries.
- You are so NOT the bitch your husband made you out to be.
- Yes, you're definitely nicer when you're drunk. Maybe you should keep a bottle in your desk?
- Your girlfriend's a really good dancer. Have you gotten her a pole for at home yet?
- No, I'm pretty sure the tinsel would look better on you than the tree.
- I'd love to hear "O Tannenbaum" sung again . . . in German. Reminds me of the rallies in the old country.

➤ Do your kids ever ask why Santa smells like gin and onion dip?

➤ I agree. This picture of you and the boss is gonna rock on Facebook.

➤ Hey, you put a candy cane in a martini and you can barely taste the booze!

➤ You know what would be cool? Taking off our clothes and wrapping ourselves in gift paper. Wanna?

➤ When I screw up at this time of year, I just say, "Santa made me do it!"

William Phelps, marking exam papers shortly before Christmas one year, came across a curious answer to one of his more perplexing questions: "God only knows the answer to this question. Merry Christmas." Phelps returned the paper with the following annotation: "God gets an A, you get an F. Happy New Year!"

~•~

Kevin: I got myself for Secret Santa. I was supposed to tell somebody, but I didn't.

Michael: Presents are the best way to show someone how much you care. It's like this tangible thing that you can point to and say, "Hey man, I love you this many dollars worth." So Phyllis is basically saying, "Hey, Michael, I know you did a lot to help the office this year, but I only care about you a homemade oven mitt's worth." I gave Ryan an iPod.

Everyone wants the iPod. It's a huge hit. It is almost a Christmas miracle.

Dwight: Michael keeps bragging about his iPod. but you know what? Two paintball lessons with someone as experienced as I am is worth easily, like, two grand.

Michael: Unbelievable. I do the nicest thing that anyone has ever done for these people, and they freak out. Well, happy birthday, Jesus. Sorry your party's so lame.

—THE OFFICE

~•~

6 Ways to Drive Your Cube Mate Crazy

1. Wear a Santa suit all the time. Deny you're wearing it.

2. Paint your nose red and wear antlers. Constantly complain about how you never get to join in on the games.

3. Make conversation out of Christmas carols. (i.e., "You know, I saw Mommy kissing Santa Claus underneath the mistletoe last night.")

4. Put on a fake white beard and insist that all your colleagues "give it a yank."

5. Ring jingle bells every fifteen minutes, saying "Every time a bell rings an angel gets their wings."

6. Steal a life-size nativity scene and display it in your cubicle. When your officemate asks, tell her, "I had to let them stay here, there's no room at the inn."

It's a Job, OK?

- ➢ There are currently 78 people named S. Claus living in the United States—and one Kriss Kringle.

- ➢ December is the most popular month for nose jobs.

- ➢ Weight of Santa's sleigh loaded with one doll for every kid on earth: 333,333 tons.

- ➢ Number of reindeer required to pull a 333,333-ton sleigh: 214,206—plus Rudolph.

- ➢ Average wage of a mall Santa: $11 an hour.

- ➢ With real beard: $20.

- ➢ To deliver his gifts in one night, Santa would have to make 822.6 visits per second, sleighing at 3,000 times the speed of sound. At that speed, Santa and his reindeer would burst into flames instantaneously.

- ➢ Of all mall Santa applicants, 7% were discovered to have criminal backgrounds.

- ➢ Among Americans, 4% believe Santa drives a sports car in the off-season, but 25% thinks he drives an SUV.

A guy wakes up after the annual office Christmas party with a pounding headache, cotton-mouthed and unable to recall the events of the preceding evening.

After a trip to the bathroom, he makes his way downstairs, where his wife puts some coffee in front of him. He moans, "Tell me what happened last night. Was it as bad as I think?"

"Worse," she says, her voice oozing scorn. "You made a complete ass of yourself. You succeeded in antagonizing the entire board of directors, and you insulted the president of the company, right to his face."

"He's an asshole. Piss on him."

"You did," comes the reply. "And he fired you."

"Well, screw him!" says the man.

"I did. You're back at work on Monday."

Christmas is over and business is business.
—FRANKLIN PIERCE ADAMS

Symbols
(SANTA)

IN WHICH THE AUTHOR EXPLORES THE RITES AND
FOIBLES OF THE HOLIDAYS AND FINDS THEM RICH FOR
MOCKING—EXAMINES THE LEGEND OF THE FAT MAN
IN THE RED SUIT—PUTS THE CONCEPT TO THE LITMUS
TEST—AND ULTIMATELY FINDS IT LACKING

THE ONE QUESTION THAT has always plagued the holidays, the conundrum wrapped inside an enigma surrounded by a mystery is . . . Is Santa Claus real? Nobody knows, but man, a lot of people do believe in him. An overweight Caucasian guy with a long white beard, dressed in funny red clothes who is fond of children.

And, they argue, if he wasn't real, would we still be talking about him? Hard to counter.

So what DO we know? Some say that before he became Santa as we know him, he may have been Saint Nicholas, a fourth-century bishop. If this is correct, Santa is now 1,700 years old. Looks good, right? How has he lasted so long?

Could he be . . . happy? Well, he has the best job in the world. He works ONE day a year. He travels. He eats lots of cookies. And when he does actually work, he's got a million elves to help him, then spends the rest of the year chillin' with the Mrs. . . . Sweet deal, no?

Hey, but not everybody believes, and here's the classic snark to prove it.

Beginning with Santa in infancy, and ending with the Tooth Fairy as the child acquires adult teeth. Or, plainly put, beginning with all the possibility of childhood, and ending with an absolute trust in the national currency.
—CHUCK PALAHNIUK

++

Why is *Santa* an anagram for *Satan?* I mean, besides the fact that both have the same amounts of the same letters. Just consider the many other similarities between the two figures: Both of them are red, both of them like to laugh, both of them give presents to children, and both of them are kings of an ungodly underworld of unspeakable horror and suffering. Coincidence? I THINK NOT.
—SAM LOGAN

+++

You better watch out. You better not cry. You better
not pout, I'm telling you why . . . Santa Claus might put
a cap in your ass.
—CRAIG FERGUSON

••

My father was so cheap that one year he told us Santa
didn't come because he wears red and we lived
in a Crips zone.
—A. J. JAMAL

•••

I never believed in Santa Claus because I knew no white
man would be coming into my neighborhood after dark.
—DICK GREGORY

••

Let me see if I've got this Santa
business straight. You say he wears
a beard, has no discernible source of
income, and flies to cities all over the
world under cover of darkness? You
sure this guy isn't laundering illegal
drug money?
—TOM ARMSTRONG

•••

~•~

Calvin: This whole Santa Claus thing just doesn't make sense. Why all the secrecy? Why all the mystery? If the guy exists, why doesn't he ever show himself and prove it? And if he doesn't exist what's the meaning of all this?
Hobbes: I dunno. Isn't this a religious holiday?
Calvin: Yeah, but actually, I've got the same questions about God.
—CALVIN AND HOBBES

~•~

Santa Claus wears a Red Suit,
He must be a communist. And a beard and long hair,
Must be a pacifist.
What's in that pipe that he's smoking?
—ARLO GUTHRIE

••

I played Santa Claus many times, and if you don't believe it, check out the divorce settlements awarded my wives.
—GROUCHO MARX

•••

Three wise men? You must be joking.
—ANONYMOUS

✦✦

"You mean you're going to send the same form letter
to the Great Pumpkin, Santa Claus and the Easter
Bunny?" "Why not? These guys get so much mail they
can't possibly tell the difference . . . I bet they don't
even read the letters themselves! How could they?
The trouble with you, Charlie Brown, is you don't
understand how these big organizations work!"
—LUCY, *CHARLIE BROWN*

✦✦✦

The Supreme Court has ruled that they cannot have a
nativity scene in Washington, D.C. This wasn't for any
religious reasons. They couldn't find three wise men
and a virgin.
—JAY LENO

✦✦

I stopped believing in Santa Claus when I was six.
Mother took me to see him in a department store, and
he asked for my autograph.
—SHIRLEY TEMPLE

✦✦✦

Top 10 Responses to the Gift of a Holiday Sweater

10. Hey! Now there's a gift!
9. Well, well, well . . .
8. Boy, if I had not recently shot up 4 sizes, that would've fit.
7. This is perfect for wearing around the basement.
6. I hope this never catches fire! It is fire season, though. There are lots of unexplained fires.
5. If the dog buries it, I'll be furious!
4. I love it—but I fear the jealousy it will inspire.
3. Sadly, tomorrow I enter the Federal Witness Protection Program.
2. Damn . . . I got this the year I vowed to give all my gifts to charity.
1. I really don't deserve this.

The 3 Stages of Man

> ➢ He believes in Santa Claus.
>
> ➢ He doesn't believe in Santa Claus.
>
> ➢ He is Santa Claus.

Santa and his reindeer land on top of an outhouse.
Santa looks around for a moment and then yells "No,
Rudolph! I said the SCHMIDT house!"
—ANONYMOUS

++

~+~

Q: How do elves greet each other?
A: Small world, isn't it?

~+~

Santa Claus? You have to look very carefully at a
man like this. He comes but once a year? Down the
chimney? And in my sock?
—IRWIN COREY

+++

Santa Pickup Lines

- ➢ Wanna see my twelve-inch elf?

- ➢ I've got something special in the sack for you!

- ➢ Ever make it with a fat guy with a whip?

- ➢ I know when you've been bad or good, so let's skip the small talk.

- ➢ Some of my best toys run on batteries. . . .

- ➢ Interested in seeing the "North Pole"? (Well, that's what the Mrs. calls it.)

- ➢ I see you when you're sleeping . . . and you don't wear any underwear, do you?

- ➢ Screw the "nice" list—I've got you on my "naughty" list!

- ➢ Wanna join the "Mile High" Club?

- ➢ That's not a candy cane in my pocket, honey. I'm just glad to see you. . . .

~✦~

*Fran: Look, Gracie! Santa took a bite out of the
cookies we left him.*
Grace: I didn't know Santa wore red lipstick.
*Fran: The man gets out of the house once a
year. Live and let live.*
　　　　—THE NANNY

~✦~

Jesus never put up a tree and exchanged gifts, or
left cookies out for Santa. He never made a harried
last-minute trip to the mall, or spent Christmas Eve
cursing at a toy he couldn't put together. He celebrated
Passover. So if you want to be more like Jesus,
pass the matzo.
　　　　—DREW CAREY

✦✦

Ways to Confuse Santa

> ➤ Instead of milk and cookies, leave him a salad, and a note explaining that you think he could stand to lose a few pounds.

> ➤ While he's in the house, go find his sleigh and write him a speeding ticket.

> ➤ Leave him a note explaining that you've gone away for the holidays. Ask if he would mind watering your plants.

> ➤ While he's in the house, replace all his reindeer with exact replicas. Then wait and see what happens when he tries to get them to fly.

> ➤ Keep an angry bull in your living room. If you think a bull goes crazy when he sees a little red cape, wait until he sees that big red Santa suit!

> ➤ Build an army of mean-looking snowmen on the roof, holding signs that say "We hate Christmas" and "Go away Santa."

> ➤ Leave a note by the telephone telling Santa that Mrs. Claus called and wanted to remind him to pick up some milk and a loaf of bread on his way home.

➢ Throw a surprise party for Santa when he comes down the chimney. Refuse to let him leave until the strippers arrive.

➢ While he's in the house, find the sleigh and sit in it. As soon as he comes back and sees you, tell him that he shouldn't have missed that last payment, and take off.

➢ Leave a plate filled with cookies and a glass of milk out, with a note that says, "For The Tooth Fairy. :)" Leave another plate out with half a stale cookie and a few drops of skim milk in a dirty glass with a note that says, "For Santa. :("

➢ Take everything out of your house as if it's just been robbed. When Santa arrives, show up dressed like a policeman and say, "Well, well. They always return to the scene of the crime."

➢ Leave out a copy of your Christmas list with last-minute changes and corrections.

➢ While he's in the house, cover the top of the chimney with barbed wire.

➢ Leave lots of hunting trophies and guns out where Santa's sure to see them. Go outside, yell, "Ooh! Look! A deer! And he's got a red nose!" and fire a gun.

> Leave Santa a note explaining that you've moved. Include a map with unclear and hard-to-read directions to your new house.

> Set a bear trap at the bottom of the chimney. Wait for Santa to get caught in it, and then explain that you're sorry, but that from a distance he looked like a bear.

> Leave out a Santa suit, with a dry-cleaning bill.

> Paint "hoof-prints" all over your face and clothes. While he's in the house, go out on the roof. When he comes back up, act like you've been "trampled." Threaten to sue.

> Instead of ornaments, decorate your tree with Easter eggs.

Our local department store had two Santas—one for regular kids and one for kids that wanted ten toys or less.
—MILTON BERLE

✦✦

Aren't we forgetting the true meaning of Christmas, the birth of Santa?
—BART SIMPSON

✦✦✦

Santa Claus goes by many names . . . Kris Kringle,
Saint Nicholas, Mastercard . . .
—PHYLLIS DILLER

++

You can't fool me. There ain't no sanity clause.
—CHICO MARX, *A NIGHT AT THE OPERA*

+++

I can't help it. There's something about a man in a
Santa Claus suit that just drives me absolutely crazy!
I don't know. Maybe it's— it's the warmth of all that
RED HOT SWEATY flannel, set against the austere
coldness of those BLACK PATENT LEATHER
boots . . . OR maybe it's because those rosy cheeks and
twinkling eyes bespeak a passion that is about to erupt
from a man who just spent a COLD LONELY year
cooped up with a pack of dwarfs! I'm not sure. All I
know is the sight of a Santa sets my body aflame with
unbridled desire!
—BLANCHE, *THE GOLDEN GIRLS*

++

Mae West once designed a special Christmas card featuring a nude shot of herself with the following caption: "Come up and see me sometime. Merry Christmas, Mae West."

Her publicist, objecting to the card's nudity, substituted a design of his own featuring a shot of an exhausted Santa Claus. The caption? "Santa comes but once a year—too bad!"

Santa is a genuinely sinister figure. Think about it: a single, old man watches everything little children do, because he wants to know which are the naughty ones? People have been hounded out of town by mobs for far less.

—JULIAN BAGGINI

•••

There are anthropologists who claim that Santa's irrepressible hilarity and ability to fly are the result of midwinter revelers ingesting large quantities of magic mushrooms. Ho, ho, ho! Indeed!

—WILL SELF

••

Department Store Santa's Pet Peeves

> ➤ Kids who refuse to believe that it's fruitcake on your breath and not gin.
> ➤ When the last guy to use the beard leaves bits of his lunch in it.
> ➤ Even with the costume, people keep recognizing you from Crime Watch.
> ➤ Parents who get all uptight when you offer their kids a swig from your hip flask.
> ➤ Enduring the taunts of your old buddies from drama school.
> ➤ Those dorks in the Power Rangers costumes get all the babes.
> ➤ Kids who don't understand that Santa's been a little jittery since he got back from 'Nam.
> ➤ Two words: lap rash.

Top Reindeer Games

- ➤ Strip poker with Mrs. Claus

- ➤ Attach the Mistletoe to Santa's Ass

- ➤ Spin the Salt Lick

- ➤ Crapping down the chimneys of nonbelievers

- ➤ Moose or Dare

- ➤ Bait-and-Shoot Elmo

- ➤ Turn-Frosty-Yellow-from-50-Paces

- ➤ Scare the Holy Crap Out of the Airline Pilot

- ➤ Convince the Elves to Eat Raisinets

- ➤ Pin the Tail on Santa's Big Fat Animal-Abusing Ass

- ➤ Hide the Venison Sausage with Vixen

- ➤ Elf Tossing

- ➤ Sniff the Tail on the Donkey

- ➤ The "Rudolph the Shitfaced Reindeer" Drinking Game

A little boy had just received a brand-new bike for Christmas and was riding it down the street. He stopped at a red light next to a police officer on a horse.

The officer asked the boy, "Did Santa bring you that new bike?" And the boy replied, "Yes!"

"Well, it looks like Santa forgot to put reflectors on the back of your bike," said the police officer. "The next time I see you, there better be reflectors on your bike!"

The little boy replied, "Yes, sir," and then he asked, "Officer, can I ask you a question?"

"Yes," replied the officer.

"Did Santa bring you that horse?" asked the boy.

"Yes he did . . . why?" said the officer.

The boy replied, "Cos if I ever get a horse, I'm going to ask Santa to put the dick under the horse instead of on top!"

Top 10 Reasons to Like Hanukkah

1. No roof damage from Santa and his reindeer.
2. Never a silent night when you're among your Jewish loved ones.
3. If someone screws up on their gift, there are seven more days to correct it.
4. You can use your fireplace.
5. Naked Spin-the-Dreidel.
6. Fun waxy buildup on the menorah.
7. No awkward explanations of virgin birth.
8. Cheer? Optional.
9. No Irving Berlin songs.
10. Betting Hanukkah gelt on candle races.

Q: Why was Santa's little helper depressed?
A: Because he had low elf-esteem.

On a busy day twenty-two thousand people come to visit Santa, and I was told that it is an elf's lot to remain merry in the face of torment and adversity. I promised to keep that in mind.

—DAVID SEDARIS

‥

Ja Rule once explained why he preferred artificial Christmas trees. "I had a real tree once," he recalled. "You got to water them, keep the base filled up all the time. Can't let it get dry." Why not? "Say you're smoking next to it—it might ignite."

Smoking next to the tree? "Some people like gold on their tree, some people like silver," he explained. "I like some special greenery on mine. Truthfully, weed's the perfect ornament. You can have such a good time on Christmas, you know? Have a smoke or two while you open your gifts."[7]

---

[7] Ah, the true spirit of Christmas.

Why a Christmas Tree Is Better Than a Man

1. A Christmas tree is always erect.
2. Even small ones give satisfaction.
3. A Christmas tree stays up for twelve days and nights.
4. A Christmas tree always looks good— even with the lights on.
5. A Christmas tree is always happy with its size.
6. A Christmas tree doesn't get mad if you break one of its balls.
7. You can throw a Christmas tree out when it's past its sell-by date.
8. You don't have to put up with a Christmas tree all year.

Let's be naughty and save Santa the trip.
—GARY ALLAN

✦✦✦

Tinsel is really snakes' mirrors.
—STEPHEN WRIGHT

✦✦

Why a Christmas Tree Is Better Than a Woman

1. A Christmas tree doesn't care how many other Christmas trees you have had in the past.
2. Christmas trees don't get mad if you use exotic electrical devices.
3. A Christmas tree doesn't care if you have an artificial one in the closet.
4. A Christmas tree doesn't get mad if you break one of its balls.
5. You can feel a Christmas tree before you take it home.
6. A Christmas tree doesn't get mad if you look up underneath it.
7. A Christmas tree doesn't get jealous around other Christmas trees.
8. A Christmas tree doesn't care if you watch football all day.

~•~

Q: *How are a Christmas tree and a priest alike?*
A: *They both have ornamental balls.*

~•~

❦

Santa was getting ready for his annual trip . . . but there were problems everywhere.

Four of his elves got sick, and the trainee elves did not produce the toys as fast as the regular elves, so Santa was beginning to feel the pressure of being behind schedule. Then Mrs. Claus told Santa that her mom was coming to visit. This stressed Santa even more.

When he went to harness the reindeer, he found that three of them were about to give birth and two had jumped the fence and escaped. More stress.

When he began to load the sleigh, one of the boards cracked, and the toy bag fell to the ground and the toys scattered. Frustrated, Santa went into the house for a cup of apple cider and a shot of rum.

When he went to the cupboard, he discovered that the elves had hidden the liquor, and there was nothing to drink. In his frustration, he accidentally dropped the cider pot, and it broke into hundreds of little pieces all over the kitchen floor. He went to get the broom and found that mice had eaten its straw end.

Just then, the doorbell rang, and irritable Santa trudged to the door to open it, and there was a little angel with a great Christmas tree.

The angel said, very cheerfully, "Merry Christmas, Santa. Isn't it a lovely day? I have a beautiful tree for you. Where would you like me to put it?"

Thus began the tradition of the little angel on top of the Christmas tree.

A Snarky Night Before Christmas

I'VE ALWAYS HAD A problem with this Clement C. Moore tale.[8] Maybe it was the fact that it's been parodied ad nauseam, with everything from a Hemingway version to Aliens. Or maybe it's that the whole poem is just one big lie.

I've taken the liberty of snarking it and placing my interpretation within the pages of an 1848 version of the book. Welcome to the twenty-first century!

---

[8] If he even actually wrote it. No one really knows.

VISIT FROM SANTA CLAUS.

TWAS the night before Christmas, when all through the house
Not a creature was stirring, not even a mouse;
The stockings were hung by the chimney with care,
In hopes that St. Nicholas soon would be there;
The children were nestled all snug in their beds,
While visions of sugar-plums danced in their heads;
And Mamma in her 'kerchief, and I in my cap,
Had just settled our brains for a long winter's nap;

OK. The night before is nothing BUT stirring. Last-minute wrapping, killing yourself to put that "thing" together, cooking, cleaning, "getting ready" . . . all in the name of celebration. "Stockings hung with care"? They're just a receptacle for extra loot. Tack 'em up and be done with it. "St. Nick" will come, regardless.

"Sugar-plum fairies?" That's probably the six-pack of Coke and the extra-large box of Now and Laters talking. And nestled? If you can get a kid to sleep on Christmas Eve, you should rent yourself out for parties.

When out on the lawn there arose such a clatter,
I sprang from the bed to see what was the
matter.
Away to the window I flew like a flash,
Tore open the shutters and threw up the sash.

The moon on the breast of the new-fallen snow,
Gave the lustre of mid-day to objects below,
When, what to my wondering eyes should ap-
pear,
But a miniature sleigh, and eight tiny rein-deer,
With a little old driver, so lively and quick,
I knew in a moment it must be St. Nick.

More rapid than eagles his coursers they came,
And he whistled, and shouted, and called them
by name;

The noise of such a clatter woke you up . . . but not the kids? You did use drugs, didn't you?

And as for eight reindeer, please tell me Santa had a pooper-scooper on him. What, why not? Do the little house elves have to do his dirty work? Where is Heriome Granger when you need her? Is he above the law? I don't think so.

Um, could it have been anybody but St. Nick? I mean, has there been a rash of thieves in the neighborhood that land on the lawn in the bright moonlight with eight tiny reindeer? Of course it's St. Nick, you moron.

" Now, *Dasher !* now, *Dancer !* now, *Prancer* and *Vixen !*

On, *Comet !* on, *Cupid !* on, *Donder* and *Blitzen !*

To the top of the porch ! to the top of the wall !

Now dash away ! dash away ! dash away all !"

As dry leaves that before the wild hurricane fly,

When they meet with an obstacle, mount to the sky ;

So up to the house-top the coursers they flew,

With the sleigh full of Toys, and St. Nicholas too.

And then in a twinkling, I heard on the roof,

The prancing and pawing of each little hoof —

Now he's screaming out reindeer names? Really? Hasn't he ever heard of the clicker method for training animals? Jeez. Nick, Nick, not so loud. The neighbors are still pissed from the Halloween blowout. Keep it down, will ya?

This Moore guy uses some flowery text, no? "As dry leaves fly"? Somebody's been taking Poetry 101, now, haven't they? And maybe I'd be OK with the whole thing if it were only toys being delivered. But we all know there are a ton of polyester socks, remainder books, and inedible fruitcake on that miniature thing.

Did he say he "twinkling" or "tinkling" on the roof? I just had the damn thing re-shingled. Between Nick relieving himself and the reindeers doing their reindeer thing, it's gonna need a lot more work. It just never stops, does it? Again, I have to wonder how the kids are still asleep.

As I drew in my head, and was turning
     around,
Down the chimney St. Nicholas came with a
     bound.
He was dressed all in fur, from his head to his
     foot,
And his clothes were all tarnished with ashes
     and soot ;
A bundle of Toys he had flung on his back,
And he looked like a pedlar just opening his
     pack.
His eyes — how they twinkled ! his dimples,
     how merry !
His cheeks were like roses, his nose like a
     cherry !
His droll little mouth was drawn up like a
     bow,
And the beard of his chin was as white as the
     snow ;

Aw, man, the chimney too? Couldn't he just jimmy the lock on the front door?

Fur, Santa . . . fur? I guess he didn't realize that global warming has really taken the chill out of winter around here.

And of course, he's tarnished and covered with soot.

Eyes a-twinkle and merry dimples too? Either he's a cabbage-patch kid, or he's been adding a little sumthin' sumthin' into the milk and cookies we left for him . . . it sounds like Santa might have a tiny little drug problem too.

The stump of a pipe he held tight in his teeth,

And the smoke it encircled his head like a
wreath ;

He had a broad face and a little round belly,

That shook when he laughed, like a bowlfull
of jelly.

He was chubby and plump, a right jolly old elf,

And I laughed when I saw him, in spite of
myself,

A wink of his eye and a twist of his head,

Soon gave me to know I had nothing to dread ;

He spoke not a word, but went straight to his
work,

And fill'd all the stockings ; then turned with a
jerk,

Hey, there's no smoking in here! What, you couldn't light up outside? No, you had to drag it in here so that the whole house STINKS of pipe smoke. Sure, go ahead, laugh, but you're getting a letter from my lawyer.

Wait a minute . . . that doesn't smell like tobacco? Santa!

"Chubby and plump"? He's fat. All year he eats and smokes and drinks. Works one night of the year—eating cookies and milk the entire time, I might add. Nice.

I'm really digging the nose/chimney thing. Great trick. Way better than the I Dream of Jeannie method, with the crossed arms and all. Although I gotta say, she kind of did more with less, if you know what I mean.

And laying his finger aside of his nose,

And giving a nod, up the chimney he rose;

He sprang to his sleigh, to his team gave a
whistle,

And away they all flew like the down of a
thistle.

But I heard him exclaim, ere he drove out of
sight,

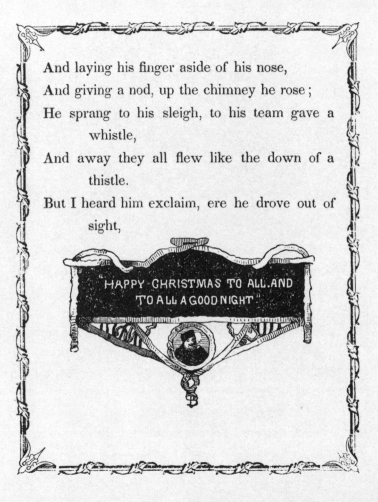

HAPPY CHRISTMAS TO ALL, AND
TO ALL A GOOD NIGHT.

Enough already.

First yelling and now whistling . . . you don't stop, do ya, Nick? You think you're at home with no rules? Well, you're not.

So, good riddance and get off my roof and out of my yard.

And yeah, yeah, yeah . . . Happy Christmas to you too.

Libations
(ALCOHOL)

SPEAKING DIRECTLY TO A MODE OF SURVIVAL—
EXCUSING POOR BEHAVIOR WITH THE BOTTLE—RULES
FOR LIQUOR—HOW DIFFERENT RELIGIONS DEFINE
DRINKING—INTRODUCING SEVERAL METHODS OF
IMBIBING—WITHOUT REGARD FOR RESULTS—THE
MEANS TO AN END

EAT, DRINK, AND BE MERRY. Yep, nothing takes the edge off the holidays (or puts and keeps it on) like the copious intake of libations, booze, hootch, hair of the dog.

So drink up. And snark away. You can always blame it on the bottle.

I have something which makes it all bearable, the presents, the in-laws, other people's children, your own children, the games, the noise, the mess, the ridiculous meals. It consists of one part French cooking brandy, one part Irish whiskey and four parts fresh milk. The hard part is remembering to put milk instead of water into your ice cube trays the night before. Drink the mixture immediately on rising, while others are having breakfast or throwing up behind the snowman.

—KINGSLEY AMIS

Rules for Holiday Drinking

Stay busy, get plenty of exercise, and don't drink too much. Then again, don't drink too little.
—HERMAN "JACKRABBIT" SMITH-JOHANNSEN

✦✦✦

Always do sober what you said you'd do drunk. That will teach you to keep your mouth shut.
—ERNEST HEMINGWAY

✦✦

The proper behavior all through the holiday season is to be drunk. This drunkenness culminates on New Year's Eve, when you get so drunk you kiss the person you're married to. Christmas at my house is always at least six or seven times more pleasant than anywhere else. We start drinking early. And while everyone else is seeing only one Santa Claus, we'll be seeing six or seven.
—P. J. O'ROURKE

✦✦✦

Drink will take the place of parlor games and we shall all pull crackers and probably enjoy ourselves enough to warrant at least some of the god-damned fuss.
—NOËL COWARD

In the old days, it was not called the Holiday Season;
the Christians called it "Christmas" and went to
church; the Jews called it "Hanukkah" and went to
synagogue; the atheists went to parties and drank.
People passing each other on the street would say
"Merry Christmas!" or "Happy Hanukkah!" or (to the
atheists) "Look out for the wall!"

—DAVE BARRY

++

I'm not a drinker; my body won't tolerate spirits, really.
I had two martinis New Year's Eve and I tried to hijack
an elevator and fly it to Cuba.

—WOODY ALLEN

+++

Thanksgiving is the day when you turn to another
family member and say, 'How long has Mom been
drinking like this?' My mom, after six Bloody Marys
looks at the turkey and goes, "Here, kitty, kitty."
—DAVID LETTERMAN

••

The first thing in the human personality that dissolves
in alcohol is dignity.
—ANONYMOUS

•••

O God, that men should put an enemy in their
mouths to steal away their brains! that we should,
with joy, pleasance, revel, and applause, transform
ourselves into beasts!
—WILLIAM SHAKESPEARE

••

My grandmother is over
eighty and still doesn't need
glasses. Drinks right out of
the bottle.
—HENNY YOUNGMAN

•••

I like to keep a bottle of stimulant handy in case I see a snake, which I also keep handy.
—W. C. FIELDS

+++

The chief reason for drinking is the desire to behave in a certain way, and to be able to blame it on alcohol.
—MIGNON MCLAUGHLIN

++

I'll stick with gin. Champagne is just ginger ale that knows somebody.
—HAWKEYE IN *M*A*S*H*

+++

I drink only to make my family seem interesting.
—DON MARQUIS (WITH ARTISTIC LICENSE)

++

The harsh, useful things of the world, from pulling teeth to digging potatoes, are best done by men who are as starkly sober as so many convicts in the death-house, but the lovely and useless things, the charming and exhilarating things, are best done by men with, as the phrase is, a few sheets in the wind.
—H. L. MENCKEN

+++

Brandy, n. A cordial composed of one part thunder-and-lightning, one part remorse, two parts bloody murder, one part death-hell-and-the-grave and four parts clarified Satan.
—AMBROSE BIERCE

+ + +

There ain't no devil, it's just god when he's drunk.
—TOM WAITS

+ +

I do like Christmas on the whole. . . . In its clumsy way, it does approach Peace and Goodwill.
But it is clumsier every year.
—E. M. FORSTER

+ + +

Christmas is a time for remembering. So that's me, f**ked.
—OZZY OSBOURNE

+ +

You've Had Too Much Holiday Cheer When . . .

1. You strike a match and light your nose.
2. A duck quacks—and it's you.
3. You tell your best joke to a plant.
4. The fish bowl looks like a punch bowl.
5. You mistake the closet for a bathroom.
6. When you leave a party, the door locks behind you.
7. You ask for an ice cube and put it in your pocket.
8. While mimicking the biggest bore in the room, you realize it's actually you in the mirror.

Remember: During the holidays, you're not drunk . . . you're mulled. And people always notice when you linger under the mistletoe.
—ROBERT MCCAMMON

♦♦

First you take a drink, then the drink takes a drink, then the drink takes you.
—F. SCOTT FITZGERALD

♦♦♦

Come, woo me, woo me; for now I am in a holiday
humor, and like enough to consent.
—WILLIAM SHAKSPEARE

••

I have the same resolution every year: I decide to drink
heavily. Because I know I can do it, which will build up
my self-esteem.
—BETSY SALKIND

••

Christmas Fact
➤ "Wassail" comes from the Old Norse *ves
heill*—to be of good health. This evolved
into the tradition of visiting neighbors
on Christmas Eve and drinking to their
health . . . until you pass out. It's also the
sound you make as you projectile-vomit a
heady mix of nog, gin, wine, and beef jerky.

New Year's is a harmless annual institution, of no
particular use to anybody save as a scapegoat for
promiscuous drunks, and friendly calls and
humbug resolutions.
—MARK TWAIN

•••

Christmas Toasts

- ↪ May your Christmas be full of friends and booze and no socks.

- ↪ A merry Christmas to all my friends except two or three.

- ↪ To a fruity, flatulent Christmas!

- ↪ Merry Stressmas!

- ↪ Forgive us our Christmases as we forgive them that Christmas against us.

There is a remarkable breakdown of taste and intelligence at Christmastime. Mature, responsible grown men wear neckties made of holly leaves and drink alcoholic beverages with raw egg yolks and cottage cheese in them.
—P. J. O'ROURKE

✦✦✦

Nourishment
(FOOD)

IN WHICH THE AUTHOR REVELS IN THE CONSUMPTION
OF MASS QUANTITIES OF SUGAR AND CARBS—
REVEALS THE OPENING OF OLD WOUNDS BETWEEN
MOUTHFULS OF MASHED POTATOES—AND MAKES
THE DISCOVERY OF BRUSSEL SPROUTS WRAPPED IN A
NAPKIN AND ROLLED INTO A BALL—FOOD AS A MEANS
OF SURRENDER

THE HOLIDAYS ARE ABOUT EATING. End of story. For weeks on end, there are sweets and pies and chocolate and turkeys the size of doghouses and stuffing and wheelbarrows of potatoes and . . . and . . . and . . . all as far as the eye can see. And all devised to make you forget about logic in the name of celebration.

The Christmas dinner might be both the worst and the best part of the holiday. More so than the everyday preparation of food, this dinner takes so much work . . . hours/days/months of buying, mixing, prepping, and is gone in a matter of minutes. Except for leftovers. Lots and lots of leftovers.

You can't make everyone happy. "What happened to the carrots you used to make with the little marshmallows?" "This turkey's too big/not big enough/too dry/not cooked enough . . . " "Why didn't you do your usual stuffing?"

"I hate . . . [pick one—or more] yams/cranberries/
brussel sprouts/figs."

People who spend the year watching their weight let
it all go during the season.

"Hey, it's the holidays. You're dead a long time. I'm
gonna just eat what I want and diet be damned. I'll start
again in January." Which you never do.

Snark can help.[9]

Nothing says holidays like a cheese log.
—ELLEN DEGENERES

✦✦✦

Thanksgiving is a magical time of year when families
across the country join together to raise America's
obesity statistics. Personally, I love Thanksgiving
traditions: watching football, making pumpkin pie, and
saying the magic phrase that sends your aunt storming
out of the dining room to sit in her car.
—STEPHEN COLBERT

✦✦

---

[9]   Snark as a digestive.

I finally finished eating the gingerbread man. The last
thing I ate was his foot and on the way down my gullet,
he actually kicked me.
—GROUCHO MARX

+++

Hey kids! I made your favorite cookies: Christmas
trees for the girls and bloody
spearheads for Bart.
—MARGE, *THE SIMPSONS*

++

Thanksgiving, man . . . Not a good day to be my pants.
—KEVIN JAMES

+++

The best way to thaw a frozen turkey? Blow in its ear.
—JOHNNY CARSON

++

The Christmas dinner was fairly ghastly . . . the
turkey was passable, but there were no sausages with
it, no rolls of bacon and no bread sauce, and the roast
potatoes were beige and palely loitering.
—NOËL COWARD

+++

The turkey has practically no taste except a dry fibrous flavor reminiscent of warmed-up plaster of Paris and horsehair. The texture is like wet sawdust and the whole vast feathered swindle has the piquancy of a boiled mattress.
—WILLIAM CONNOR

+++

Last Thanksgiving, I shot my own turkey. It was fun. Shotgun going, "Blam! Blam!" Everybody at the supermarket just staring. Why track them when you know where they are?
—KENNY ROGERSON

++

I love Thanksgiving turkey . . . it's the only time in Los Angeles you see natural breasts.
—ARNOLD SCHWARZENEGGER

+++

A number of other truly remarkable things show up in holiday dinners, such as . . . pies made out of something called "mince," although if anyone has ever seen a mince in its natural state, he did not live to tell about it.
—P. J. O'ROURKE

+++

Consider Christmas—could Satan in his most malignant mood have devised a worse system of graft and buncombe than the system whereby several hundred million people get a billion or so gifts for which they have no use, and some thousands of shop clerks die of exhaustion while selling them, and every other child in the Western world is made ill from overeating—all in the name of Jesus?
—UPTON SINCLAIR

◆◆◆

Dear Lord, I've been asked, nay commanded, to thank Thee for the Christmas turkey before us . . . a turkey which was no doubt a lively, intelligent bird . . . a social being . . . capable of actual affection . . . nuzzling its young with almost human-like compassion. Anyway, it's dead and we're gonna eat it. Please give our respects to its family. . . .
—BERKE BREATHED

◆◆

Christmas Pudding: festering gobs of adamantine suet that the Brits think of as fun food.
—JOE QUEENAN

◆◆

You may be an undigested bit of beef, a blot of mustard,
a crumb of cheese, a fragment of underdone potato.
There's more of gravy than of grave about you, whatever
you are!

—CHARLES DICKENS

✦✦✦

Grammy Moon's famous plum duff is a pudding boiled in
a cloth bag. She had a secret ingredient. She'd soak it for
hours in rum, then ignite it in a blinding flash. As soon as
she came out of the kitchen with no eyebrows, we knew
dessert was ready. To this day, the smell of burning hair
puts me in the holiday spirit. Merry Christmas!

—DAPHNE, IN *FRASIER*

✦✦

I celebrated Thanksgiving in an old-fashioned way. I
invited everyone in my neighborhood to my house, we
had an enormous feast, and then I killed them and took
their land.

—JON STEWART

✦✦

Women used to make great mince pies and fake
orgasms. Now we can do orgasms, but have to fake
mince pies. Is this progress?
—ALLISON PEARSON

+++

You can tell it's the Christmas season. Stores are selling
off their expired milk as eggnog.
—DAVID LETTERMAN

+++

The holidays can turn into a year of overeating. There
are some who gain 20 or 30 pounds over the year. Their
mind-set is "Why not keep going?"
—LESLIE FINK

+++

"Never, ever ask a former clergyman to say the blessing
over a holiday dinner. Not if you like your dinner
warm, anyway."
—MARY KAY ANDREWS

++

"Thanksgiving dinners take eighteen hours to prepare.
They are consumed in twelve minutes. Half-times take
twelve minutes. This is not coincidence."
—ERMA BOMBECK

+++

The Best Christmas Cake Ever

Ingredients:

1 cup butter	1 cup sugar
4 large eggs	1 cup dried fruit
1 teaspoon baking powder	1 teaspoon baking soda
1 tablespoon lemon juice	1 cup brown sugar
1 cup nuts	1 or 2 quarts of aged whiskey

Before you start, sample the whiskey to check for quality. Good, isn't it?

Now go ahead. Select a large mixing bowl, measuring cup, etc. Check the whiskey again as it might be just right. To be sure the whiskey is of the highest quality, pour 1 level cup into a glass and drink as fast as you can.

Repeat.

With an eclectic mixer, beat 1 cup of butter in a large fluffy bowl.

Add 1 teaspoon of sugar and beat the hell out of it again. Meanwhile, at this parsnicular point in time, wake sure the whixey hasn't gone bad while you weren't lookin'. Open second quart if nestessary.

Add 2 large eggs, 2 cups fried druit an'beat'til high. If druit gets shtuck in peaters, just pry the monsters loosh with a drewscriver.

Example the whikstey again, shecking confistancy, then shitf 2 cups of salt or destergent or whatever, like anyone gives a schit.

Chample the whitchey shum more.

Shitf in shum lemon zhoosh. Fold in chopped sputter and shrained nuts.

Add 100 babblespoons of brown booger or whushevers closhest and mix well.

Greash ubben and turn the cakey pan to 350 decrees. Now pour the whole mesh into the washin' machine and set on sinsh shycle.

Check dat whixney wunsh more and pash out.

Merry Cishmash!

If you're at a Thanksgiving dinner, but you don't like
the stuffing or the cranberry sauce or anything else, just
pretend like you're eating it, but instead, put it all in
your lap and form it into a big mushy ball. Then, later,
when you're out back having cigars with the boys, let
out a big fake cough and throw the ball to the ground.
Then say, "Boy, these are good cigars!"

—JACK HANDEY

++

Christmas is a major holiday. Hanukkah is a minor
holiday with the same theme as most Jewish holidays.
They tried to kill us, we survived, let's eat.

—ANONYMOUS

++

Turkey: A large bird whose flesh, when eaten on certain religious anniversaries, has the peculiar property of attesting piety and gratitude.
—AMBROSE BIERCE

••

I came from a family where gravy was considered a beverage.
—ERMA BOMBECK

•••

After a good dinner, one can forgive anybody, even one's own relatives.
—OSCAR WILDE

•••

Here I am, 5 o'clock in the morning, stuffing breadcrumbs up a dead bird's butt.
—ROSEANNE BARR

••

Every Christmas, I feel like a child. But we always get turkey.
—TERRY JONES

•••

The worst gift is a fruitcake. There is only one
fruitcake in the entire world, and people
keep sending it to each other.
—JOHNNY CARSON

◆◆

It took me three weeks to stuff the turkey.
I stuffed it through its beak.
—PHYLLIS DILLER

◆◆◆

Women have fun baking for Christmas. Jewish women
burn their eyes and cut their hands grating potatoes
and onions for latkes on Hanukkah. Another reminder
of the suffering through the ages.

◆◆

People are so worried about what they eat between
Christmas and the New Year. They really should be
worried about what they eat between the New Year
and Christmas.

◆◆◆

Can I refill your eggnog for you? Get you something to eat? Drive you out to the middle of nowhere and leave you for dead?
—CLARK GRISWOLD, *CHRISTMAS VACATION*

♦♦

We're having something a little different this year for Thanksgiving. Instead of a turkey, we're having a swan. You get more stuffing.
—GEORGE CARLIN

♦♦♦

My cooking is so bad my kids thought Thanksgiving was to commemorate Pearl Harbor.
—PHYLLIS DILLER

♦♦

You know that just before the first Thanksgiving dinner there was one wise, old Native American woman saying, "Don't feed them. If you feed them, they'll never leave."
—DYLAN BRODY

♦♦♦

Recovery
(HANGOVER)

IN WHICH THE REVELERS CONSUME MASS QUANTI-
TIES OF ANALGESIC PRODUCTS—WINCINGLY RECALL
CONVERSATIONS AND DEEDS THAT SHOULD NEVER
HAVE HAPPENED AND CAN'T BE UNDONE—AND THE
EVENTUAL OATH OF "NEVER AGAIN" IS HEARD
ONCE MORE

SWAIN SC

THE DAY AFTER . . . YOU MIGHT want to take a deep sigh of relief; but remember, the shit never ends. Now you will be looking straight into the jaws of exchange lines, longer than they ever were to buy stuff; using gift cards in stores with no inventory; boxing up the ornaments, trying to hit the "under" in the breakage betting; tossing the tree, seeing who can be first or who can be last; pulling even more fruitcake wrapped in napkins from the folds of the couch; dieting, even as the fridge is full of food gifts and leftovers.

Finally, after the last toast, it's back to work, glorious work . . . ah, sanctuary!

The day after Christmas is like the day after the senior prom, everybody asking each other, "What did you get?"

✦✦

Given the choice, where would you rather be this Christmas—in your kitchen with your hand shoved up a turkey's bottom, or somewhere as far away from tinsel, turkey, and tree as possible? Simply tell everyone you're going away, buy a boatload of TV dinners and DVDs, take the phone off the hook, close the curtains . . . and wake up on December 27th.

—BERNICE DAVISON

✦✦✦

Next to the presidency, detrimming a tree has to be the loneliest job in the world. It has fallen to women for centuries and is considered a skill only they can do, like replacing the roll on the toilet tissue spindle, painting baseboards, holding a wet washcloth for a child who is throwing up, or taking out a splinter with a needle.

—ERMA BOMBECK

✦✦

The day after Christmas: when we all have two more ugly sweaters.

—CRAIG KILBORN

✦✦

I love Christmas. I get a lot of wonderful presents I
can't wait to exchange.
—HENNY YOUNGMAN

+++

Much like sex, the event ends with a sad flatulent
realization that these things are better imagined than
enacted, better anticipated than performed.
—STEPHEN FRY

+++

Many people look forward to the New Year for a new
start on old habits. Good resolutions are simply checks
that men draw on a bank where they have no account.
—OSCAR WILDE

+++

New Year's Day: Now is the accepted time to make
your regular annual good resolutions. Next week you
can begin paving hell with them as usual.
—MARK TWAIN

++

Snarkin' the Holidays

What's the holiday season without New Year's resolutions? Over the years, you've vowed to lose weight, give up fatty foods, quit smoking, find a relationship that goes longer than a night.

None of these resolutions last. Have you ever met anyone who says "My resolution this year changed my whole life"? Me neither. Never happen, so why bother.[10]

—THE AUTHOR

~✦~

Sebastian: I was determined to have a happy Christmas.
Charles: Did you?
Sebastian: I think so. I don't remember much, and that's always a good sign, isn't it?
    —*BRIDESHEAD REVISTED*

~✦~

---

[10]   My resolution is to never write another snark holiday book.

Women get a little more excited about New Year's Eve than men do. It's like an excuse: You get drunk; you make a lot of promises you're not going to keep; the next morning as soon as you wake up you start breaking them. For men, we just call that a date.
—JAY LENO

••

A holiday is when you celebrate something that's all finished up, that happened a long time ago, and now there's nothing left to celebrate but the dead.
—ABRAHAM POLONSKY

•••

Cancel the kitchen scraps for lepers and orphans, no more merciful beheadings, and call off Christmas!
—THE SHERIFF OF NOTTINGHAM

••

New Year's Resolution: To tolerate fools more gladly, provided this does not encourage them to take up more of my time.
—JAMES AGATE

•••

The only way to spend New Year's Eve is either
quietly with friends or in a brothel. Otherwise,
when the evening ends and people pair off,
someone is bound to be left in tears.

—W. H. AUDEN

✦✦✦

Next to a circus, there ain't nothing that packs up and
tears out faster than the Christmas spirit.

—KIN HUBBARD

✦✦

New Year's Eve, where auld acquaintance be forgot.
Unless the tests come back positive.

—JAY LENO

✦✦✦

Yesterday, everybody smoked his last cigar, took his last drink, and swore his last oath. Today, we are a pious and exemplary community. Thirty days from now, we shall have cast our reformation to the winds and gone to cutting our ancient shortcomings considerably shorter than ever.

—MARK TWAIN

◆◆◆

Have a Rama-Hana-Kwaz-Mas. And remember . . . it ain't over until the fat angel sings!

◆◆

In Conclusion

DONE. OVER. FINI. FINITO. Basta. End of story.

You did it. You got through it, with only a few minor scrapes and scratches . . . basically unscathed. The Super Bowl and Valentine's Day are on their way.[11] The tree is gone (or should be); everything has been exchanged, boxed, stored . . . forgotten until next year, when we will take it all out and do it again. And remember . . . only 352 shopping days left!

Hey, where'd I put my new gun?

♦♦♦

---

[11] Gotta get through Chinese New Year, though.

Acknowledgments

I WISH TO HANG UP stockings and spin the dreidel for the following people:

Mom – who never actually gave me a dreidel (gelt and guilt, yes, dreidel, no), but gave me lots and lots of love; Suzanne, Kristine, Barry, John William, and Sarah – who remind me how much fun the holidays can be; Mark, James, and Miss O – all extraordinary secret Santas. The elves at the Owl; Santa's helpers at Skyhorse; my editor, Ann, who has carefully guided me through Snark Past, Future, and Present; and Rosalind, the best present Christmas morning can bring.